A Crabtree Branches Book

★ TOP HORSE BREEDS ★

SHIRE

Kerri Mazzarella

Crabtree Publishing
crabtreebooks.com

T0026246

School-to-Home Support for Caregivers and Teachers

This high-interest book is designed to motivate striving students with engaging topics while building fluency, vocabulary, and an interest in reading. Here are a few questions and activities to help the reader build upon his or her comprehension skills.

Before Reading:

- *What do I think this book is about?*
- *What do I know about this topic?*
- *What do I want to learn about this topic?*
- *Why am I reading this book?*

During Reading:

- *I wonder why...*
- *I'm curious to know...*
- *How is this like something I already know?*
- *What have I learned so far?*

After Reading:

- *What was the author trying to teach me?*
- *What are some details?*
- *How did the photographs and captions help me understand more?*
- *Read the book again and look for the vocabulary words.*
- *What questions do I still have?*

Extension Activities:

- *What was your favorite part of the book? Write a paragraph on it.*
- *Draw a picture of your favorite thing you learned from the book.*

TABLE OF CONTENTS

HISTORY

The Shire horse is the largest horse **breed** in the world and one of the rarest. They **originated** from England in the mid-eighteenth century.

DID YOU KNOW?

The Shire horse gets its name from an area in England known as the shires.

The Shire's **bloodline** comes from the "Great Horse" of **medieval** England. These large, strong horses were used to carry knights in heavy armor into battle.

The massive Shire was originally used for transportation and farming. The Shire Horse Society was formed in 1878 to set breeding guidelines and keep a record of Shires.

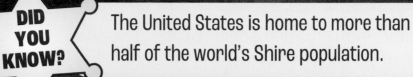

DID YOU KNOW? The United States is home to more than half of the world's Shire population.

The Shire horse was first brought to the United States in 1853. Today the Shire horse is considered an **endangered** breed.

CHARACTERISTICS

Shire horses have tall, muscular builds. They have broad shoulders, thick legs, and large hooves.

DID YOU KNOW?

In 1924, a pair of Shires pulled 50 tons (45 metric tons). That's heavier than a semitruck!

The Shire has a long, arched neck, a long, lean head, and large eyes. One characteristic that sets them apart from other breeds is the beautiful feathering on their lower legs.

Sometimes referred to as a gentle giant, the Shire horse has a sweet, calm personality. They are good with other animals and people.

Shires are very smart and are hard workers. They are part of the **coldblood** group of horses. Despite their large size, Shires are great horses for beginning riders.

SIZE AND COLOR

The massive size of the Shire horse is a sight to see. Their height ranges from 16 to 18 hands. They are the tallest horse breed.

DID YOU KNOW?

A hand is a unit of measurement used to describe the height of a horse. One hand is equal to 4 inches (10.2 cm).

Shires weigh between 1,800 and 2,400 pounds (816 and 1,089 kg). They were bred for strength and pulling heavy farm equipment.

The most common colors for Shires are black, bay, gray, or brown. They often have white markings on their faces and legs.

Shires have thick **manes** and tails. Unlike other horse breeds they have hairy lower legs! The hair on their legs is called feathers.

CARE AND FEEDING

Like all breeds, Shire horses require daily care, attention, and shelter. The average lifespan of a Shire is 25 to 35 years.

DID YOU KNOW?

A Shire's feathery legs will need to be dried properly after bathing to avoid skin irritation and infection.

Daily **grooming** and yearly veterinary visits are important for the Shire's overall health. Bathing and brushing your horse on a regular basis, as well as checking its hooves, will keep it healthy and clean.

17

Shires need more food than the average horse because of their large size! Their diet should include a mix of hay, oats, barley, and other grains.

It is important to have plenty of fresh water available for the Shire. They can consume up to 30 gallons (114 L) of water a day!

USES, JOBS, AND EQUIPMENT

The Shire horse was originally used for tough jobs that often involved heavy pulling. They were valuable to the transportation and farming industries for many years.

In the 1800s, Shire horses were primarily used for farm work, towing **barges**, and pulling carriages. Today they are still used on some small farms, as well as in the logging industry, on police forces, and for tourist carriage rides.

The Shire horse works well at many jobs. They are great for riding lessons for beginners, trail riding, and therapeutic riding programs.

saddle cloth

saddle

stirrups

helmet

It is important to have proper **horse tack** and safety equipment when dealing with any horse. They are strong, powerful animals that can cause serious injuries if you are not careful.

bridle

bit

reins

step stool

COST

The cost of a **purebred** Shire can vary depending on factors such as age, gender, bloodline, color, and training. Shire horses can cost from $2,000 to $20,000.

foal

DID YOU KNOW?

Male horses are called stallions, female horses are called mares, and baby horses are called foals.

Owning a horse can be expensive. A Shire horse will cost more than other horse breeds. Due to their size, they will eat more, drink more, and require a little extra care.

Feeding your horse will cost around $2,000 each year. Yearly costs for routine veterinary care and vaccinations for your horse are around $750.

DID YOU KNOW?

Other expenses to consider are grooming products, horse hoof maintenance, and riding equipment.

Housing will be the greatest expense for a Shire and can cost from $2,000 to $6,000 a year. The total cost of owning a Shire can be up to $10,000 each year.

THE G.O.A.T.s

A horse named Sampson was the greatest Shire of all time. Born in 1846 and later renamed Mammoth, he was the tallest and heaviest horse ever recorded. He was 21.25 hands tall and weighed 3,360 pounds (1,524 kg).

Another famous Shire horse was Goliath. At more than 19 hands tall, he was the Guinness World Record holder for tallest horse in 2000.

Goliath meets miniature horse Bluebell, June 1985

GLOSSARY

barge (BARJ): A large, flat-bottomed boat used to carry goods on rivers and canals

bloodline (BLUHD-lahyn): The ancestors of an animal

breed (BREED): A particular type of animal

coldblood (KOHLD-blud): A group of large, powerful horse breeds that are calm in nature and are often used to do heavy work

endangered (en-DAYN-jerd): An animal that is in danger of dying out

grooming (GROOM-ing): The practice of brushing and cleaning the coat of a horse, dog, or other animal

horse tack (HORS tak): The equipment used to handle and ride a horse

mane (MAYN): The long, thick hair on the head and neck of a horse

medieval (med-EE-vuhl): Relating to the Middle Ages, a period in European history from 500–1500

originated (or-IH-jin-ayt-ed): Began to exist or appear

purebred (PYOOR-bred): Having parents of the same breed

INDEX

WEBSITES TO VISIT

www.thesprucepets.com/learn-about-the-shire-horse-breed-1886127

http://ihearthorses.com/equine-411-all-about-the-shire-horse-breed

https://www.britannica.com/animal/Shire-horse

ABOUT THE AUTHOR

Kerri Mazzarella lives in South Florida with her husband, four children, and two dogs. She loves horses and has always wanted to own one. Her daughter has taken horseback riding lessons for many years. She hopes you enjoy learning about different breeds of horses as much as she does!

Written by: Kerri Mazzarella
Designed by: Kathy Walsh
Series Development: James Earley
Proofreader: Melissa Boyce
Educational Consultant: Marie Lemke M.Ed.

Photographs: Shutterstock Cover & Title pg: Alla-V, benchart; Background and Border: benchart; p 4: Neil Bussey; p 5: kontrymphoto; p 6: SandrasKnipserei; p 7: Alla-V; p 8: SandrasKnipserei; p 10: Julia Shepeleva; p 11: jean.cuomo; p 12: 1000 Words; p 14: SandrasKnipserei; p 16: Alla-V; p 17: Inc; P 18: Wirestock Creators; p 20: @Wiki; p 23: Inc; p 25: Colleen Ashley: p 26: hedgehog94; p 27: Paul Maguire; p 28: @Wiki; p 29: Trinity Mirror / Mirrorpix / Alamy Stock Photo

Crabtree Publishing

crabtreebooks.com   800-387-7650
Copyright © 2024 Crabtree Publishing

Printed in the U.S.A./072023/CG20230214

Published in Canada
Crabtree Publishing
616 Welland Ave.
St. Catharines, Ontario
L2M 5V6

Published in the United States
Crabtree Publishing
347 Fifth Ave
Suite 1402-145
New York, NY 10016

Library and Archives Canada Cataloguing in Publication
Available at Library and Archives Canada

Library of Congress Cataloging-in-Publication Data
Available at the Library of Congress

Hardcover: 978-1-0398-0942-0
Paperback: 978-1-0398-0995-6
Ebook (pdf): 978-1-0398-1101-0
Epub: 978-1-0398-1048-8